Indigo Blues

Rachel Lynn Aubry

BookLeaf Publishing

Presentation by *BookLeaf Publishing*

Web: www.bookleafpub.com

E-mail: info@bookleafpub.com

ISBN: 978-93-95890-58-8

First edition 2022

Why Oh Why?

Why oh why can't I sing when lyrics flower
inside my brain, I dance to symphonies in my
dreams
Why oh why can I not dance like the
choreography within me
Why oh why am I not pretty when my heart is so
beautiful
Why oh why am I a fashionista when all the
clothes don't fit me
Why oh why do I want to debate and be a
speaker when I can't even say the letter R
clearly
Why oh why do I have an artist eye when my
hand won't draw well at all
Why oh why can't I lie when all I do is lie to
others and myself
Why oh why am I seen as a hater and all I want
to do is love
Why oh why am I seen as sad when all I do is
laugh
Why oh why am I sad when I seem to laugh at
everything
Why oh why does no one understand me when I
understand everyone else

Why oh why is no one my true friend when I am
no one's fake friend
Why oh why do I have a story to tell when I
can't put it into words
Why oh why do I overthink when I don't even
understand simple things
Why oh why do I know so much about
important things but can't put into words the
importance of it
Why oh why do I like night time but have to
have an early bed time
Why oh why am I this way
Why oh why am I fat prejudice when I am fat
myself
Why oh why do I want a boyfriend when I don't
even talk to boys
Why oh why is Instagram and Pinterest filled
with quotes of being yourself when in reality no
one seems to want that
Why oh why do I hate the people that are like
me the most
Why oh why am I this way
Why oh why does it have to be this way

The Feeling Of My Brain Melting

What are the words to describe the feeling of my
brain melting?
There might not be feeling centers in my brain
But I feel like I am a bobble head with TOO big
a head weighing me down
Someone keeps flicking at my head to see what
it will take till my head pops OFF!
My struggle is entertainment
Just laugh it up, one day I hope you LOSE your
mind too
A pile of brick sitting attached to my neck
The world on my shoulders
Steam coming out of my ears
Tears dry up on my face
Words go in one ear and leak out the other
The thought process is not on the right track
today
It went ahead and crashed
The choo-choo train needs more gas
It's atop a hill teetering on the edge, another inch
forward and it will slide down
I keep LOSING my grip
I am on the downhill track
All the traction I have made is lost

Losing ground
Losing a grip on reality
Without my brain as a working machine
My body CRUMBLES, legs fall asleep
My body aches
My brain: my engine, overheats
My head shakes trying to get it back in place
What do I do?
I am shutting down
Reverting inside is my default
FALL asleep
Maybe when I wake it will be alright
Till then GOODNIGHT

Dreams Unlived

My punishment if I could guess
Is written on my lips
On the tip of my tongue
Scorched in my throat
I know in my soul
What would make my soul sing
It lives in my dreams
A thought too far away to grasp
It dances in my dreams and flits away
Leaving me no clue how to pursue
What do I do?
I live my dreams through other means
Written words not stories told
Collages created not my true art expression
Poetry not music
I am not giving up
My heart will sing
I will dance to my heart's content
I find any way to express myself

Shame

Shame shame I know your name, but you do not
know mine!
You never will, I am above the fool's game.
I will never look at you the same.
I am doing just fine; self-respect is my baseline.
You help no one with all your blame.

Silence Is Deadly

Tears roll down slowly
Not a heavy crier
No one notices
A single tear escapes
Screaming silently for someone to notice
No one does
They misunderstand the anger
It is all pain and fear
Not one to draw attention
My ranting is only because I don't want to cry
right now
That's for the privacy of my room
I have just a little too much control of my
emotions
But not enough to stop them
Just delay the mental break
Delay, delay
Put a pause on my life
Shut down mentally
Curl up into a ball

Starlight

Night is all consuming
Enveloping the noise and bustle of the day
Only the thousand-year-old remnant star is alive
in the night
They shine bright while the Darkness surrounds
them
By far the brightest light in all the land
The dark can't not dim the light
It stands tall and bright
Throughout the night
No matter the plight

Kill, Rip, Tear

I just want to tear at myself, my skin is itchy,
prickly
Apply more pressure to my dry eyes
Rip out my oily tickling hair
Always something out of place niggling at me.
Back'n forth, side to side trying to find a
comfortable spot
JUST make it STOP
I am crying from defeat.
To many angry thoughts overwhelming me.
Scratching, rationalizing to myself just one more
scratch.
Just one more will relieve me.
What a big fat lie.

Caged Beast

Eyes burning from tears unshed
Trying so hard to keep them from falling
Body aching
Hands shaking
Tremendous urge to bang my head against the
wall
Screaming in my head
This is me holding back
The monster in me is in pain
Ready to destroy anything in its path
Dangerous amongst friend and foe
A monster wounded is more dangerous than a
monster at its full strength
No one know that I am holding back
A caged beast gnawing at itself
Risking my own hide I don't know why
Maybe I know I am the only cage I won't truly
destroy
No place to escape
So I must sing a lullaby
Bring myself back to harmony
The beast and I

Toxicity

I don't need a guy to go back-and-forth with "I
hate you, I love you"
I do it with myself; I do it to myself. I love
myself enough I might be a narcissist.
I hate myself Ugh... Why am I this way?
It's a never-ending cycle, yes-no, love-hate.
It never ends, ugly-pretty, healthy-sick,
skinny-fat, good-bad, smart-stupid,
friendfull-friendless.
This relationship is toxic
My most important relationship hurts me but I
can't break it off.
It's a pattern of behavior, a way of life but it
doesn't feel like I am living.

Pure Gold

Life a beautiful masterpiece of cycles, bigger
pictures schemes to get you to where you need
to be when it really matters.
Would you rather have the pleasure of a golden
hour or a golden lifetime?
So, my life didn't go as planned, my middle
school to high school experience not something I
would brag about.
Always wished for more, to feel whole.
Found the truth of fullness deep within me, in
my dreams and people that get me.
Said goodbye to the random collection of people
I grew up with.
A golden lifetime of memories to make.

Inner Child

All the colors of a rainbow
Sees play in every opportunity
A model, actress, ninja, pirate, anything is
possible
Cuddles, cotton candy sweater, fuzzy forts,
laughing until I am blue
Teacher, tea parties
Having fun, lighthearted creative girl
Connected to you more than most
Playing right along with you no matter my age
Dancing in the middle of the street at night
Jumping on my bed
Layering unlikely clothes to create the ultimate
outfit
I don't care how I look as long as it brings me
joy
Silly spontaneous fun

Dancer

I am a dancer.
I feel the music pull my feet to where they need
to be.
Gently guiding the sway of my hips.
Each muscle moving in accordance with the
melody.
It is an intuitive dance; I feel it in my cells.
I can feel the music thrumming, building, almost
ready to crash like a wave when the beat drops.
I jump, soaring, riding the wave.
Coasting on crescendos, always in tune with the
music.
It feels deliciously freeing to fly, lightly
bouncing on my toes, twirling along with a
lyrical story.
I am part of the story, an instrument to express
the motions of emotion felt.

Truth

My body is a tuning fork.
Truth resonates so deeply.
I break out into smiles to news my soul knows is
wonderfully true.
Each shiver and knee jerk reaction tell a story.
So, without knowing what the rest of my story
holds I know it is a good one.
I am here, happy, smiling all silly just thinking
about it.
I just know more has been assigned to my name.
Tingling, light touches electrify my body.
I can hear the little fairies laughing in the wind
and the birds laughing with me in their chirps.
I can't help but smirk at how everything is
working out.
What a wonderful time to be alive.

On The Edge

A letter to future me.
You are me and I am you.
You are just farther along in time.
What's it like to, be you?
Who have you met; what new friends do you have?
Don't tell me.
I am anticipating the day but I can wait.
It is a delicious kind of torture to be on the edge.
Leaning forward into my future but also unsure
if I am pushing myself too fast.
Day after day I am settling into this new me and
expanding at the same time.
I think it is so great to be in love with change.
To greet each day newly as I discover what it
means to be alive today.
I love living newly each day like a brand-new
outfit or fresh car smell.
Testing out the way these brand-new shoes fit.
Yesterday's clothes just never quite fit.
How colorful you must be, future me.

Dance With Me

A letter to my future lover.
The one who makes my soul sing and laugh so hard.
I trust we will dance in our unique way.
A great partner is one who knows how to dance on your own, to catch me and lift me up.
I trust you to see to you own hopes and dreams as I see to mine.
I know that we align in life themes, values and when we are together, I gleam.
I knew my worth early on and reach for the stars.
They reach back for me.
I know I am reaching for you, and in time we will be face to face.
A whole new dance in person shall commence.
For all our elegant glory you can be sure I will step on your toes.

When, Where, Why…How?

Seeing numbers
Seeing patterns
Don't know what to do
Tell me straight
Don't make me wait
Heard it in a dream
What was it again?
Deja vu please
Need a trigger
Make me remember
Hearing a calling
Far far in the distance
Too bad I have terrible hearing
Dream it, believe it, see it
I am seeing that vision
Too bad I don't wear my glasses to sleep
Too bad I have sucky vision

Surgeon

Carve out time.
Carve out space in your life.
Slice and dice away at the myths and limiting
beliefs.
Whittle away at the parts of your life that you do
not like.
Cut according to what is best for you.
Doctors cut us open to heal us and take out the
rotten parts of ourselves.
Stitch yourself and you are as good as new,
better in fact.

Birds Eye View

I am so high up standing alone on top a
mountain peak observing the world below.
It makes me feel not so alone, but I am.
I have the bird's-eye view, I can see the whole
world but they can't see me.
They think they can.

SHIT DAY

I AM HAVING A SHITTY FUCKIN DAY
I AM SO FUCKIN HAPPY YAY
I DON'T GIVE A FUCK WHAT YOU SAY
WHY DOES LIFE HAVE TO BE THIS WAY?
KARMA WILL MAKE YOU PAY
I AM FEELING A BIT RISQUE IN WHAT I
SAY
I WILL FIGHT TILL YOUR ON YOUR
KNEES READY TO PRAY
ARE YOU SURE YOU WANT TO PLAY?
RUN AWAY NOW BECAUSE I WILL BE
THE ONE WALKING AWAY

Born For This

When the moment comes, I will give it my all.
I was born for this.
Signed up for this experiment to create and live
a life of joy.
Why support the doubt and fear, the dream
stealer, mind killer?
Ready to risk my hide but it's not really a risk
when I am betting on myself.
Investing in my health.
Being my best self, left all that was not me.
So, when that moment comes it was made for
me.
Deep breath, I gather all the magic with in me
and I begin making magic with my words.
My presence fills the room.

Home

Home where art thou?
Are you with my parents, but they don't always provide me what I need, the comfort that I seek?
Are you with my friends the people I can laugh with and share secrets but they don't know everything about me?
Are you in my room, the walls that seem to be closing in even when all my treasures line the shelves?
Are you in my body the place where my soul is housed?
Home is where the heart is, so yes. It is where the love is for me unconditionally.
You can find those moments in your friends and your family and your music but it's only moments.
The backlash used to be so cold when I relaxed into the moment and forgot others were not my permanent home.
Their approval I do not need.
Physically impossible to embrace me the way I would in those tenuous moments.
But it always comes back to this vessel, yet it is not just my body where my home is.

For a long time my body didn't feel like home it
was a prison holding me here.
My heart was caged by hurt, shame, jealousy,
hate and fear.
It was such small home to live in.
Maybe that's why I would escape and live in
music and stories.
A place to live free of the hurt and judgments.
My body is my palace, my home, my physical
expression of myself.
I can decorate it with colors and wear my
favorite scents.
I can feel the rain, wind and love on my skin.
I am in harmony with my body, my mind and
my soul, this is home.